The Birthday Present

"Coloured Bedtime StoryBook"

By

Vinaykumar Kasju

Illustrated by

Devendra Pandey

ILLUSTRATED & PUBLISHED
BY
E-KİTAP PROJESİ & CHEAPEST BOOKS

www.cheapestboooks.com

 www.facebook.com/EKitapProjesi

ISBN: 978-625-6308-97-8

Copyright, 2024 by e-Kitap Projesi
Istanbul

Categories: Adventure, Community, Problem Solving
Country of Origin: Laos
Cover: © Cheapest Books
License: CC-BY-4.0

For full terms of use and attribution, http://creativecommons.org/licenses/by/4.0/

Contributing: Devendra Pandey

© **All rights reserved**.

Except for the conditions stated in the License, no part of this book shall be reproduced or transmitted in any form or by any means, electronic or mechanical, including photocopy, recording or by any information or retrieval system, without written permission form the publisher.

About the Book

Maya the Tortoise tries everyday to get to school in time, but ends up being late. She needs a bicycle. But where ever will she find a bicycle for a tortoise? Read on to see what she receives as a birthday present.

The Birthday Present
Vinaykumar Kasju
Devendra Pandey

"Mama, please buy me a bicycle! I can reach school faster than the rabbit if I have a bicycle. And I'll beat everyone on the exam, too!" Maya told her mother.

"Okay dear, I will buy you a bicycle on your birthday," her mother said. "But where can I get a bicycle for a tortoise? Do you know?"

Maya had seen humans travel as fast as birds on their bicycles. But, try as she might, she couldn't remember ever having seen a bicycle made for a tortoise. But surely there was one!
"I will ask my friends at school tomorrow," Maya said. "And I'll let you know!"

Maya lived in Kachuwo village near the Fewa lake. She was a very hard-working tortoise. She never missed school, but she was always late for school because her school was so far from her house.

Everybody called her Tiny Turtle Late-Late. Nobody likes being called names. Maya didn't like it, either.

Maya would have liked to reach school before her friends did, but her legs were short! No matter how fast she ran, she would always be late for her English class. And what was why she did not get good marks in English.

Today, also she reached school late.

"May I come in, Teacher?" she asked as she stood at the door.

"It's Tiny Turtle Late-Late!" the class laughed. The teacher looked angry, but allowed her to enter the classroom.

At the end of the class, the teacher made Maya stand in front of the class. "Maya, you are always late!" the teacher said. "You were late yesterday, and you were today. If you do not come to class on time, you will not be allowed to enter the classroom. Is that clear?"

Maya almost burst into tears. "But I'm not late on purpose! My house is across the lake. So no matter how I try to be on time, I cannot. What can I do teacher? My legs are short. I want to be on time for school and study well."

Maya's class laughed at her. Her teacher asked them to stop. She said to Maya, "You are right. But when you come late to class, it disrupts everyone. Let's discuss this matter with the principal."

Maya stopped her teacher. "Please do not do that! My mother has promised to buy me a bicycle on my birthday. I can then be on time for school." Big Cat asked, "But when is your birthday, Maya?"

Maya did not know when her birthday was. Maya hesitated.

The teacher went to the wall. She checked the calendar and said, "Maya, your birthday is tomorrow!"

Maya said happily, "Is it really tomorrow, Teacher? Maybe mother had forgotten."

Maya turned towards her class. "But my mother does not know where to buy a bicycle for a tortoise. Do any of you know?"

Even her teacher did not know where to get a bicycle for tortoise! She said, "Maya, since your birthday is tomorrow, we will try to find out where you can get a bicycle. Then we will come to your house and tell your mother. Do not forget to treat us with selroti* tomorrow. Okay?"

*A doughnut like sweet

Maya was so happy about the plan! She wanted to get home as soon as possible. She couldn't wait to her mother about her birthday the next day, and about her whole class coming to her house.

"Mother!" Maya called from the door. "It's my birthday tomorrow! My class is coming to our house!" Mother was cooking selroti in the kitchen.

Mother came out of the house to greet her daughter. "Of course I remember your birthday! But it seems like my daughter had forgotten."

"So you must already have found my bicycle!" Maya cheers.

Mother sat down sadly. "I asked others where I can get a tortoise bicycle for you, but nobody knows. I don't know where to find one. But we will keep trying. We find it one day."

Maya was not sad. "My teacher has said she will help us! Don't worry mother."

Then Maya and her mother cooked selroti, malpua, and other sweets for the next day.

Early the next morning, Maya's mother wished her happy birthday. Then Maya went to the lake and took a bath.

She met some ducklings at the lake. They wished her a happy birthday, too. One duckling gave Maya a shiny shell. Maya thanked the duckling and told them about the bicycle. The ducklings were surprised.
'Can you really find a tortoise bicycle?" They asked.

Maya's class had arrived by the time she reached home.

 "Happy Birthday Maya," they sang and clapped.

Mother served Maya and her friends yummy dishes to eat. Before they began to eat, Maya's teacher said, "Maybe we should first gave Maya her birthday gift?"

Maya's class gave her a package wrapped with a red ribbon. Maya wondered what could be inside the box!

"Maybe it's a box of sweets or a toy," she thought.

Maya's teacher said, "We reached Pokhara city in search of a bicycle, but we couldn't find one. At last, this is what we saw."

Maya opened the box. The box contained something that Maya had never imagined. It was a pair of shoes with wheels!

"You can now wear this and reach school on time," her class cheered. "Hooray!"

Maya's eyes filled with tears of happiness. "I am so grateful to all my class and my teacher! With these wheel shoes on, I will always be at school on time. I am going to do so well on the upcoming exams!"

Everybody clapped. Maya's mother cheered as well. She said, "Perhaps I can buy Maya a computer on her next birthday."

Everybody began to eat and enjoy the sweets. Meanwhile, Maya took her wheel-shoes and began to dream of the next morning.

End of the Story

www.ingramcontent.com/pod-product-compliance
Lightning Source LLC
LaVergne TN
LVHW070452080526
838202LV00035B/2808